HURRICANE

HURRICANE

My Story of Resilience

SALVADOR GÓMEZ–COLÓN

Norton Young Readers

An Imprint of W. W. Norton & Company
Independent Publishers Since 1923

To all the young people who want to build a better future and those who have already begun.

Series edited by Dave Eggers, Zainab Nasrati, Zoë Ruiz, and Amanda Uhle.

For information about permission to reproduce selections from this book, write to Permissions, W. W. Norton & Company, Inc., 500 Fifth Avenue, New York, NY 10110

For information about special discounts for bulk purchases, please contact W. W. Norton Special Sales at specialsales@wwnorton.com or 800-233-4830

Manufacturing by Lake Book Manufacturing
Book design by Hana Anouk Nakamura
Production manager: Beth Steidle

ISBN 978-1-324-01665-6

W. W. Norton & Company, Inc., 500 Fifth Avenue, New York, N.Y. 10110
www.wwnorton.com

W. W. Norton & Company Ltd., 15 Carlisle Street, London W1D 3BS

0 9 8 7 6 5 4 3 2 1

CONTENTS

INTRODUCTION 1

Chapter 1 **Calm** 7

Chapter 2 **Storm** 17

Chapter 3 **Aftermath** 27

Chapter 4 **Plan** 39

Chapter 5 **Momentum** 45

Chapter 6 **Commitment** 55

Chapter 7 **Action** 65

Chapter 8 **Recovery** 71

Chapter 9 **Light** 77

CONTINUE THE DISCUSSION 85

GET INVOLVED 90

TIMELINE 92

AUTHOR'S ACKNOWLEDGMENTS........... 97

EDITORS' ACKNOWLEDGMENTS 103

INTRODUCTION

Zainab Nasrati, Zoë Ruiz, and Dave Eggers

One of the best ways to understand complicated issues is through the story of a person who lived at the center of it. If you want to learn about what would drive teenagers to fight for young women's rights to education in Burundi, why not read the story of someone directly involved? This is what this series is all about: letting young people—who have seen and lived through recent history—tell their stories.

It's important to understand other people's struggles, especially people who live in different places or come from different backgrounds than you do. Our hope with this book series is that by hearing one person's story, our readers will learn about many people's struggles and think about what we can do together to help make the world better.

Teenagers like Malala Yousafzai and Greta Thunberg became iconic for standing up for what they believe is right. Other teens, not yet as well known, have also stepped up to make a difference. When Adama Bah was a teenager, she was falsely accused of criminal activity because she is Muslim. When Gilda Temaj was only sixteen, she had to leave her home in Guatemala and make her way alone to the United States. Now that she's a college student, Gilda is studying to become a lawyer so she can help others who seek safe haven in the United States.

The I, Witness books will bring you stories of ordinary kids and teens like you who have faced extraordinary challenges in their lives. Their stories are exciting and surprising. At times they are sad, and at others they are joyful. We hope that you will consider your own life and your own story as you read. Is your life very similar to the author's? Or very different? Is there a problem in the world or in your life that you would like to help solve?

In this book, you'll meet Salvador Gómez-Colón, who lived through Hurricane Maria in Puerto Rico in 2017. After the storm left the island devastated, he jumped into action, helping hundreds of his fellow islanders with basic needs. We admire Salvador's drive to help others, and think that all of us can learn from what he faced and what he achieved. Some of us will never endure a hurricane, but all of us will do well to remember the determination Salvador showed in finding help for his neighbors, even when others doubted him. As readers ourselves we were heartened and inspired by Salvador's story, and we hope you will be, too.

HURRICANE

CHAPTER 1

Calm

Eighteen days before Hurricane Maria, I turned fifteen years old. The morning of my birthday, I woke up to blue balloons all over the apartment and a happy birthday sign on the dining table. Every year, my mom decorated the apartment, and I looked forward to it more than any other present.

It may seem like a small thing, but her decorations meant a lot to me. After school, I celebrated my birthday by having a late lunch with my best friends at a Chinese restaurant. That weekend, I went to my grandparents' beach apartment with my dad on the east coast of Puerto Rico. My family has owned that apartment since before I was born, and as a child I had spent countless summers there with my cousins in what we call our "Family Camp." I reflected on both those years and turning fifteen years old. It all felt so monumental.

At the time, I lived in Condado, a neighborhood in the capital city of San Juan. I went to school, where I enjoyed photography, had swim practice every day, and attended Model United Nations competitions on Fridays and Saturdays. My parents had separated when I was five years old, so I split time between my mom's house and my dad's. A few years after the divorce, I went from being an only child to having two stepsisters once my mom remarried. I loved spending time with my two stepsisters, and we got along well. I was content and lived a normal life. But after Hurricane Maria, I was forced out of normalcy. We all were.

Hurricane Maria was unlike any other storm I had seen or felt in my past. There had never been anything as destructive, so there was nothing to compare it to. In Puerto

Rico, hurricanes are part of every summer, so I have lived through quite a few. There is a hurricane almost every year, and they are usually Category 2 or Category 3 storms.

The first thing to know about hurricanes is that they are *all* destructive and that *all* the categories are powerful. Hurricanes have already passed two thresholds: tropical depression and tropical storm. Categories 1 to 3 hurricanes are manageable, though they always cause flooding, damage to buildings, and injuries. A Category 4 hurricane is a beast within itself, but there is no cap to a Category 5 hurricane. A Category 5 takes everything and devours it. It is a storm without mercy. Hurricane

Maria fluctuated between a Category 4 and Category 5. When it hit Puerto Rico, it was a Category 4 storm.

Prior to Hurricane Maria, the strongest storm that I had lived through was Hurricane Irene, and it was a Category 3 storm. I remember the chaos it had caused on the island. The powerful winds and heavy rainfall caused people to lose electricity and water. I was in second grade and everyone at school was talking about it. One of my sisters' third-grade teachers was named Irene, and after the hurricane my sister's classmates were mean to the teacher.

Politicians and the media announced Hurricane Maria was coming and said it was going to hit us hard, but they made the announcement on a Sunday, only two days before the hurricane. They had given us more warning with Hurricane Irma, a hurricane that had come two weeks earlier. Maria caught us in the dark.

On Monday I went to school, but after first period the principal sent out an email announcing that students were required to leave school and return to their homes at noon. That night, after my half day at school, I felt so anxious about the hurricane that I did not sleep.

On Tuesday, September 19, my mom, grandpa, grandma, and I prepared for the hurricane. My stepdad would have been with us, but he was in New York, and my stepsisters were with their mom. My dad stayed with my paternal grandparents to watch over them. We packed bags in case we had to leave our apartment or the building. Because we lived three blocks from the beach, we were warned there could be tsunami-like flooding, and that we might have to evacuate the building, which was the worst-case scenario.

We packed only the necessities. We each had cash, snacks, and bread. We filled up as many thermoses as possible with water because we did not know how long we would be away from the apartment if we had to leave. We put two thermoses in each of our bags. My grandparents packed their medications and my grandpa packed his old radio. I packed my asthma inhalers and a word search book for some entertainment.

After we packed, we settled in for the storm. We decided to stay in the living room because it was near the front door and we could leave immediately if we needed to. It was also safest for us there because hurricane-force winds could create a vacuum and seal the bedroom doors, making them impossible to open. We felt fortunate that no matter what happened, we had each other, the four of us.

That night, Governor Ricardo Rosselló

released a video online, saying that the disaster would be unlike any other and emphasizing the importance of unity and preparedness.

Only fifteen families lived in our building and we all knew each other. We were a tight-knit apartment building, and my family had lived there for years. Miriam was our eighty-year-old neighbor, a widow whose husband had passed away before we moved in. I imagined her feeling scared and lonely and got worried. We knocked on her door and said, "We are going to go downstairs at some point. We will knock on your door so that you can come with us, if you want." She thanked us and said she wanted to go with us.

Around nine in the evening, the wind picked up and rain started falling, and we could hear the wind roaring at the windows. Two hours passed, and I heard the shutters banging and the winds getting stronger.

I was exhausted because I had not slept the night before, and around midnight I surprisingly fell asleep on the couch. A few hours later, I woke up to chaos.

CHAPTER 2

Storm

Now, when I try to remember what happened during and immediately after the hurricane, it is a blur. I remember only certain aspects of the experience. I remember I woke up and felt groggy. I put my feet on the floor and felt that it was wet. I thought, *Nope. No way.*

I looked down. My ankles were under three inches of water. When I looked up, I saw my mom and my grandpa throwing my sheets and pillows and comforter on the floor. They were trying to soak up the water, and I stood up to help.

The water had rushed into our apartment through vents and air-conditioning units. *This hurricane has just started*, I thought. *It's only going to get worse.* I texted and called a few of my friends to check in and see how they were doing. Soon after, I had no cell service and I lost communication with them completely.

The living room, my room, and my mom's room were flooded. The air-conditioning unit was on the floor. It had just popped out because of the change in air pressure when the hurricane hit. We threw clothes onto the living room vents as water poured inside. As we tried to stop more water from coming into the bedrooms, the building started to sway.

"We need to get out of here," my mom said.

We felt the entire building shake. We knew if we got stuck up there, it would be terrible.

"It's time to go downstairs," she said.

We grabbed the bags we had prepared. We left our apartment not knowing when we were going to be able to return. I felt so many emotions at once, but mainly I felt helpless and a certain kind of vulnerability and fragility that I had never felt before in my life.

Before we went downstairs, we knocked on Miriam's door. She answered and we said, "We're going downstairs now. You should come down with us."

"Yes," she said. "Of course."

Water rushed down the stairwell, entering the building through leaks in the roof. We went downstairs to the lobby and then inside the building's gym. Eight people were already in the room. There was a middle-aged couple with their seventeen-year-old daughter and a small dog, a couple with a baby, and two elderly people.

I had never used the building's gym. I'd

only go into the gym to press a breaker switch when the elevator was acting finicky. I never would have guessed that the gym would be my salvation one day.

I had affectionately called the gym a broom closet because it was not that big. The room was about nine-by-sixteen feet. There was a treadmill, a set of weights, a small sixteen-inch TV mounted on the wall, and a window. The window had metal bars that reinforced it on the outside and on the inside. We could see what was going on outside through the glass. We saw palm trees flying through the air, and the winds lifting and moving cars. Everything was just whipping past. Everyone was scared. The baby was crying, and the small dog was barking. I was anxious and confused, and I felt like we were all so defenseless. I just kept thinking, *This is not normal. This is not normal.*

We started watching the news on the small TV. The news showed footage of trees flying and glass breaking because of the winds. Suddenly the TV went gray. We found out later that the roof of the news station had collapsed. After the TV stopped broad-casting, we started listening to my grandpa's old radio.

Before the hurricane, my grandpa used to watch TV every day, and he loved his movies. But when he could no longer watch TV during the hurricane, he resorted to listening to the radio. It became the main source of news for my family. The night of the hurricane and every night for weeks after, we listened to the radio. I called it "Grandpa's Famous Radio." I noticed that his radio seemed to bring back the past for him.

Through the glass door of the gym, we saw that people were trying to make sure the inside of the lobby was as safe as possible. The winds from the hurricane had ripped off the glass doors of the front entrance and the entrance to the parking garage. People brushed water away from the stairwell, including a sixty-year-old man and the president of our condominium association. People were trying to put a makeshift wooden panel where the glass door of the parking entrance had been.

I left the gym and went to help them. I grabbed a yellow broom and started to clear the water that was coming down the stairwell, which was right by the entrance to the gym. I did my best to sweep the water out of the building, but the wind was still roaring and my mom was scared that something would fly through the entrance of the building and injure me. "Come back in," she shouted, and I did.

I felt powerless. I was shaking so intensely that I felt like a maraca being rattled from side to side. It reminded me of being on a roller coaster, reaching the highest point and just waiting to drop. I felt weightless. I felt as if I were both clinging and falling. I felt that way from the moment I woke up and saw my family soaking up water in the apartment. I tried to focus on something else. I took out the word search book from my bag and ran through almost a hundred crossword puzzles, word searches, and diagrams.

Finally, around eight in the morning, the storm quieted. We thought, *Oh, the winds are dying down.* Thinking the storm had passed, we headed back upstairs. But the storm was about to get much worse.

CHAPTER 3

Aftermath

When we were back upstairs, we got cell signal and a call from my stepdad came through.

He said, "I'm trying to come back but am stuck here." He paused. "You guys aren't upstairs, right?"

"Yes, we are," my mom said. "We just came back up. The winds have stopped."

"No, no, no. Don't do that," he said. "Right now you're in the eye of the storm. You have to get back downstairs. Right away."

Quickly, we ran down the stairs. Soon we heard the winds start blowing harder than ever. Through the window, I saw a palm tree smash a car and power lines fall. The winds kept picking things up. Everything seemed to be flying. Finally, around eleven in the morning, the winds died down.

The hurricane had passed.

We went back upstairs through the stairwell, a cascade of water streaming down it. When we reached our apartment, my mom unlocked and opened the door. An inch and a half of water was near the front entrance, which was nowhere near a window. We rushed inside.

Our living room was like a mini-pool. There were three inches of water in the living room, everything was wet, and the wall was stained. My room was also flooded, the wooden bed frame and wooden desk were swollen with water. My mom's room was flooded, too. My sisters' room was the only one that was completely fine.

We tried to stop the water from spreading. We threw sheets and clothes on the floor so that they would soak up the water. We had a generator in our building, so we were able to use the vacuum cleaner to suck out water, too, but it was a slow-going process because the container inside the vacuum was so small. We had to throw out my bed, and my desk had already started to mold. The whole day felt long and draining. Most of it remains a blur. From around eleven in the morning to eight in the evening, we cleaned and cleared water out of the apartment. That was all we could do.

The next day, we decided to drive around town. We wanted to see what was happening beyond our apartment building. My grandpa was the most curious one of us, but my grandma felt overwhelmed. She was anxious to know how her apartment was doing, but she felt conflicted. She wanted to go outside and see what had happened, but she was afraid that what she would see would overwhelm her more than she already was.

In front of my building, I saw that someone's window had flown out with its whole frame, and glass was shattered all over the ground. It was one of many things I saw that felt surreal. We went down to the parking garage underneath the apartment building. Both the parking garage and the streets were filled with a few inches of water. In Condado, the sewage and drainage systems are notoriously bad, and after the hurricane they failed. Street signs had fallen and streetlights were not working; we would not have either of these things for eleven more months. It was not safe to drive, but we all still did. In fact, when we went out driving, there was a mass of cars on the roads.

Dirt, branches, trees, and hard-to-move debris were everywhere. The hurricane had either blown away trees or stripped off all their leaves. The streak marks on the palm trees looked like something monstrous had scratched them. I had not known it was possible that hurricane winds could burn leaves and branches. We drove by the park near my home, where, ever since I was five years old, I rode my bike, played, and celebrated birthdays. I thought of that park as my backyard. None of the thirty-foot-tall, thick trees that had surrounded the park were left standing after the hurricane. I was in a state of disbelief. My home had been torn apart. I understood then why even the government said, "We are not at all prepared for this. Just pray to God that we will survive." Storms like Maria are unconquerable.

It was very traumatic to see the wreckage. I felt uncertain, like I was hanging by a thread and did not know where to go. A part of me wanted to escape what was happening, but another part of me needed to comprehend the magnitude of the effect that Hurricane Maria had on my community and Puerto Rico.

Three days after the hurricane, I looked

out my window and noticed the sky was no longer gloomy. The sky had been cloudy, gray, and hazy from the storm and all the debris. It was the first evening since the hurricane that the sunset looked somewhat normal. The sky was bright orange against a light shade of blue, and I watched in awe.

That sunset meant something to me. I tend to get lost in my thoughts very often. My mom has always poked fun at how I can be doing work one minute and then staring out the window the next, thinking about anything from what's for dinner to the current political climate. She has also always laughed at how I go down Wikipedia holes, starting on one page and then spiraling on a ten-page journey that sparks my interest in ten new subjects.

I saw the sunset that night and thought about hope. I asked myself, *How can I take a bigger role in all this?* I had been so focused on my emotions and vulnerability, and mostly thinking about our survival up to that point.

Although the power was still out, our apartment building had a generator that would turn on at night and in the morning, but many people in Puerto Rico did not have light throughout the night. My mom made sure we only turned on one light at a time in our apartment, so that we could understand how life was for others at the time. She wanted us to be in solidarity with others in Puerto Rico.

My mom has always been compassionate and has cared for other people, and she stayed aware of what went on in our community. Since I was very young, my mom would take me to homeless shelters and food drives. If it were not for my mom, I would not have had an outward mindset or the desire to help people who were vulnerable. She helped form my perspective and my attitude. She inspired me.

My fourth-grade homeroom teacher, Ms. Yaiza, was also one of my biggest inspirations. She was an amazing role model because she was committed to kindness, positivity, and helping others. She would take all sorts of service trips. She traveled the world, visiting Southeast Asia, the Middle East, Europe, and South America. She did not make much money as a teacher and she did not come from an affluent background, but she saved all her money for travel and service trips. Everywhere she went, she would find a project that would impact someone and change their life in some way. She taught me the importance of empathy and stepping up for others.

As the sun set, I felt it represented hope leaving for so many people who were in the dark. *I need to take action*, I thought. *I cannot stay here in my home and rest on my privilege. I am going to use it for the better.*

CHAPTER 4

Plan

When I asked myself, *What do people need? What is missing?* the first thing that came to mind was light, both in the physical and emotional senses. Physically, it was unsafe to be in the dark, whether that was because someone could hurt themselves or because they belonged to a vulnerable population. The possibilities are endless in terms of accidents that people could have in the dark. I also recognized that many people without light were without hope. I was fortunate enough to be surrounded by my whole family and to have a roof over my head, a relatively stable food supply, and light in my home. Still, at times I felt lonely and hopeless. I knew others had much less. What I was feeling, many were feeling to a worse degree. I could not bear the thought of people being in the dark both physically and emotionally. There was so much pain in Puerto Rico that I wanted to brighten the island, even just a little bit.

The next morning, we went to buy bread at the community bakery, two blocks from my home. The line was huge, and armed security guards stood outside the entrance of the bakery, making sure no one stole food. One male guard carried an assault rifle and the other held a revolver. I had never seen an armed security guard at a bakery in my life. I had seen them outside police headquarters or the governor's mansion, of course, but never at the place where I bought bread and orange juice and pastries. This was how desperate things were, and the response was just another destructive effect of the hurricane.

We entered the bakery and there was a stench that overtook the smell of fresh bread. I noticed that people wore unclean clothes. I recognized people that I knew from my community wearing dirty brown shorts and stained shirts. They told me that they had no power or running water, and that they lived in flooded zones that had anywhere from six inches to three feet of floodwater. While my family lived three blocks away from the beach and above sea level, they lived closer to the beach and were below sea level. Every day, they walked through the flooded zone to buy bread.

I started thinking about the physical and emotional implications of clean clothes. I thought, *Having clean clothes is not just a commodity, it is a public health issue.* My friends were walking through water that was contaminated with sewage and bacteria, all of which remained on their clothes. It was risky to keep wearing those same clothes with all that icky stuff on them. In terms of the emotional aspects, I thought, *Who doesn't like having clean clothes? Clean clothes help you feel so much better!*

I decided I wanted to distribute solar lamps with phone chargers, and also hand-powered washing machines, and call the project "Light and Hope." It was definitely an odd combination, but I told my mom and she said, "It's definitely a *you* combination." I saw what people in my community desperately needed, and wanted to do something about it.

CHAPTER 5

Momentum

In the past I'd had ideas of things that I wanted to do in my life, but they had never felt urgent. With Light and Hope, I knew I had to take action immediately. I was committed to distributing solar lamps and hand-powered washing machines to people who needed them.

My mom said, "If you want to do this, you can't start this and then stop just because it gets hard. You have to take this to the end."

"I haven't quit anything yet," I told her. "This isn't a spur-of-the-moment decision."

"If you want to raise money and distribute these items, you have to take what you get. Because it is not a matter of *if* it gets hard, it is a matter of *when*. This will get hard and be stressful, and you will get frustrated."

My mom had always been a hard worker and a strong person. She worked to pay for her education, and she had been a single mom when I was younger. She seemed to rise up and shine through any trouble. Talking with her helped me realize that it was not just about me and my idea. It was about the people I could help. If I wanted to give them hope, I realized I had to be held accountable to them.

Once I told my mom that I wouldn't back down, she put me in contact with Neha, her friend who cofounded a nonprofit organization based in Washington, D.C., that focused on using clean energy and solar light to foster female entrepreneurship in Africa. My mom had worked in government, corporate, and nonprofit jobs and she had made a lot of friends through her work. She had met Neha through the Presidential Leadership Scholars Program. Each year the program brought together leaders to develop their skills and collaborate. Neha would be the first of many of my mom's friends to help me with my efforts. I considered my mom's ability to embrace and connect with so many people a privilege.

Since the phone connection was abysmal, my first conversations with Neha were via text message. I had never talked to her before, so I introduced myself. *Hi, this is Salvador*, I texted. *I am Marta's son*. I explained my idea to purchase and distribute solar lamps and hand-powered washing machines. I asked her, *How should I go about this?*

She answered, *You should definitely do a crowdfunding campaign.*

I asked, *What should I make my goal? Do you think I should make it $50,000?*

No, you should go big. She wrote, *If you want to impact as many people as possible, go big or go home.*

I did the math. If I wanted to impact a thousand families, it was probably going to cost me around $100 per family, between the hand-powered washing machines, the solar lamps, and shipping. We set the goal for $100,000. To this day, I still think it's a lot of money. At fifteen, I thought, *Whoa. A hundred thousand dollars is* so much *money.* I was scared I would never reach that goal.

Neha helped set up the online crowd-funding page because I had no cell signal and could only get Wi-Fi connection at school or a nearby hotel. I sent her the description and picture for the crowdfunding page via SMS text messaging. It would take up to an hour for one message to send. When she received a message, she would reply, *Okay, I got it*, and then upload it. Four days after the hurricane, the campaign went live. It felt fantastic and I felt a sense of joy, but knew I was just at the first step of a long journey.

The first day of the campaign, we raised $14,000. I thought, *We can complete this in about a week. This is fantastic!* By day three, we had raised $36,000, and I thought, *Wonderful. I am on track to complete this fundraiser in five days!* Less than a week after the campaign went live, CNN and *Teen Vogue* covered it, and then more media began to cover the story. The news coverage felt surreal. My friends went wild about it and posted about it on their Snapchats, Instagram, and other social media accounts. I refused to let it get to my head, though, and I stayed focused on the numbers.

About a week into the fundraiser, a mass shooting happened in Las Vegas. It was the biggest mass murder by one person in American history. Media attention was diverted from the hurricane, as the coverage of the mass shooting was relevant and important.

But the news stopped covering Hurricane Maria completely. People went from hearing about Puerto Rico on every news channel every night and day to not hearing about it at all. Most of the donations had come from outside of Puerto Rico because people on the island, whom I never expected to donate, were struggling. I had just surpassed $60,000, but the lack of news coverage had a negative impact on donations, and the news would not start covering the fundraiser again until months later.

Although the donations slowed down,

I received an unexpected email. The Smart Electric Power Alliance emailed me and wrote, *Hey, Salvador, we read your story and we are interested in doing an office fundraiser to raise up to $10,000.* It was an amazing surprise. When I read the email, I thought, *Just what I need.* Up until then, all the donations had come from individuals. Although I did not know it at the time, the Smart Electric Power Alliance would be the first of three companies to make major contributions.

CHAPTER 6

Commitment

A week after Hurricane Maria, our school reopened and asked students to volunteer their time. We helped clean the school and walked around the neighborhood to check in on people. Two weeks after Hurricane Maria, we started classes again. The school was trying to get back to normal even though things were anything but normal. I felt frustrated that we had classes while members of our school and the community at large were suffering.

We didn't have to wear our school uniforms because students did not have electricity or water to wash their clothes. I had a friend who would kayak to school every day because she lived in an area that was so flooded she could not walk. Many students and teachers did not have power or water, so they would come to school at five in the morning, shower, and eat breakfast. Some of them would microwave their dinners, which would be something like instant noodles, and stay at school until the library closed at five in the evening. The more the school tried to make life seem normal, the less normal life felt.

A week after the storm, my mom and I decided to go on a scouting mission. We drove to El Yunque, the only tropical rain forest managed by the U.S. Forest Service, and it looked like a fire had lit up the entire forest—the trees and their leaves were gone.

We also drove through Loíza, a coastal town, east of Condado and San Juan, and about fifteen miles away. Two weeks before Hurricane Maria, Hurricane Irma had hit Loíza hard. The town had been devastated. By the time Hurricane Maria ripped through Loíza, people still did not have power. They had gone through the second, even worse storm without a chance to recover from the first. The winds had knocked down stilts that had supported wooden houses. The storm had blown off metal roofs and ripped out windows and doors. Furniture and fridges and broken cars littered the streets. Loíza looked like a war zone and I did not want people in Loíza to be left in the dark. I decided that this would be the place where I would distribute solar lamps.

By October, the campaign had raised over $60,000, and I made my first lamp order. I called the company, spoke in my deepest voice, and said, "Hello, my name is Salvador Gómez. I would like to make an order."

The representative said, "Excuse me, is this a minor?"

I felt like I was busted. I hadn't even spoken for five seconds and they already knew I was a kid.

"Yes, I am a minor."

"What is your request?" the representative asked.

"I want to purchase five hundred units of a specific lamp," I said.

"Can I speak to an adult, please?"

The company was not used to a fifteen-year-old ordering $30,000 worth of solar lamps, and they were not going to allow me to make the purchase. I felt frustrated. I was young but wanted to be taken seriously. Although I knew my request was odd for a young person, I felt disappointed they assumed my request was some kind of joke.

My mom came on the line, started to talk to them, and we finally ordered the solar lamps.

I reached out to another of my mom's friends, who gave me suggestions about where to buy hand-powered washing machines. I found Gentlewasher, a company in the Netherlands that produced them. The washers looked like cylinders with a crank on the side. While they appeared small, each washer fit up to five pants and ten shirts inside per load!

I wanted one hundred washers in the first shipment, so I reached out to them through their website contact page, but received no response. After my third follow-up email, the founder wrote that he had received my email, and they were preparing washers for shipment. The downside was that the company was short on supply, and I would not receive them until January.

By late October, the solar lamps arrived, but there was a backlog at the ports. Customs would not expedite opening the container because I was not a registered nonprofit yet, nor a notable humanitarian organization. The container that held the lamps sat there for almost a month. I was frustrated by the bureaucracy, but I kept my promise and did not give up my mission. One of my mom's friends owned the cargo area at the airport. She offered to help, made a phone call, and moved the container of solar lamps to her warehouse. Finally, I was able to access them.

In November, I reached out to St. Regis Bahia Beach Resort, located near Loíza. I emailed them and tried my best to be professional. I explained who I was and put in all the links to the articles and interviews I had done. I wrote, *I would love to see if your business can make a contribution to support my cause.* They told me that they would donate $10,000, and I thought, *Yes! Let's go!*

I reached out to Yeidimar Escobar, a

community leader in Loíza, who worked in the municipal government, and asked her what communities I should visit. She gave me a specific orientation and the information that I needed. She also assembled a small group of ten volunteers that included her husband and son, and they let people know that we were coming to their homes in advance. Finally, I was ready to distribute solar lamps to Loíza.

CHAPTER 7

Action

On Sunday, December 3, my mom, my friend María Elisa, a seven-year-old boy—our youngest volunteer—and his mother filled our cars with solar lamps, and away we went. When we arrived in Loíza, I was disappointed to see that not much had changed. It had been three months since the hurricane hit, and the devastation looked the same as it had one week after the storm. One of the reasons Puerto Rico went into 100 percent blackout after Hurricane Maria was because its electric system had been commissioned in 1941. There had been no doubt that it would fail.

In Loíza, I distributed solar lamps by going house-to-house, visiting each home. I wanted the experience to feel personal. I did not want it to feel fake. I wanted to make sure that it was grassroots, and that people felt connected to one another. I held on to the idea that the lamps were conduits of hope.

I went to the first house and was there for ten minutes. When I came outside, my mom said, "Okay, you have to speed it up because you have two hundred houses remaining." I hadn't thought through how much time distributing the lamps would take. But I picked up my speed, and we reached two hundred households that first day.

Once we'd finished going house-to-house, someone walked up to us. He introduced himself and said, "My cousin called and told me you are giving away lamps. I need lamps, too. Can I have some?"

I said, "I'm sorry, we ran out of them today. But let me get your personal information. We will reach out to you when we distribute more."

Another person drove up to us and said, "I am from the town nearby and my cousin told me you had lamps. I live in the mountains and I really need them. Can I have some?"

Yeidimar introduced the man as Lubriel. He lived in Morovis, a mountain town about one hour away from Condado.

As my mom drove us home, I said, "Mama, there is so much need beyond this town. I cannot just stay in Loíza. I cannot do it." I realized that to make an even bigger impact, I would have to try to help more people, so I became committed to reaching more towns.

Soon after we distributed solar lamps in Loíza, Lubriel messaged me on Facebook. He explained that the community in Morovis had many people with preexisting medical conditions, families with children, and people who were elderly. "Morovis is exactly where we need to go," I told my mom.

Two days before we planned to head out to Morovis, the advance team—one of my mom's friends who used to work with her—visited the community we intended to visit to lay out a distribution plan and let people know we were coming with solar lamps. On the day we went to Morovis, it was raining. I had had an asthma attack after we visited Loíza and was still sick. My mom was worried for me, but I said, "Look, Mom. I've got to do this."

CHAPTER 8

Recovery

On December 17, my mom, two friends, and I headed to Morovis with lamps. The community we visited was isolated from the rest of Puerto Rico because their main bridge had collapsed during the hurricane and floodwaters had washed it away. The river was deep and wide, about one hundred feet across. The residents had rolled rocks into the river to form a makeshift bridge, but driving across was risky and extremely dangerous. Surges of water often came down from the mountains and flipped over cars that attempted to cross the river at a bad moment. We waited for the safest time to drive across and made it to the other side.

The town looked as though the storm had passed through recently. Unlike in Loíza, most houses here were made of concrete, but had roofs that had been made of wood. Most houses were leaky or had been torn apart and about 80 percent of them now had blue tarps for roofs. Houses were stripped of paint and left windowless. There was a ton of debris and branches in the front yards. Three months after the hurricane, Morovis still lacked power. To this day many houses in mountainous areas still have blue-tarp roofs.

An elderly woman in her nineties lived in the first home we visited. It was a tiny house, about twenty-by-ten feet. Her bed was in the front room. A woman cared for her during the day, but she was bedridden, worn down, and only had a kerosene lamp for light.

I asked her caretaker, "Does she use this kerosene lamp? Is someone with her at night?"

The caretaker replied, "She stays here alone at night and uses the kerosene lamp."

Oh my, I thought, and gave her one of our lamps.

Using a kerosene lamp is a huge risk. Kerosene can spill and burn skin even without fire; if there is fire, it will consume everything it touches. I thought about how risky it was for this ninety-year-old woman who could not get out of her bed to use a kerosene lamp. What if that bed caught fire?

On our way to another house, I saw a man in his late nineties making a pile of metal scraps in his front yard.

I said, "Sir, do you want me to help?"

He said, "Oh yes, please."

As I helped him move a piece of metal scrap, he told me he had no power, he lost his wife a few years back, and he was alone without any relatives. I gave him a solar lamp. I wanted to stay longer but had to hand out more lamps. The man's story struck me. He was lonely and felt hopeless. I wondered how much resilience this man had to have in order to survive.

I visited a home and handed a lamp to a bedridden patient who had diabetes. A few weeks later, she died because she had no way to receive her treatment. This was devastating, but as I distributed more solar lamps in this town and other towns, it would not be my only gut-wrenching experience. Only months later would I understand and grasp all that I had seen.

CHAPTER 9

Light

Six months after Hurricane Maria, we were still dealing with its destruction when the media started covering Puerto Rico again. CNN reported on my fundraiser a second time and mentioned that I had already made a big impact by reaching eight hundred households. While individual donations came back in, I also received a $10,000 donation from SOMOS Community Care, a group of doctors based in New York.

I decided to partner with them for a distribution in Naranjito, a town that had experienced many landslides because of the hurricane. Although it was only twenty miles away, the route there had many twists and turns, and it took us more than an hour to arrive. Because I shared the distribution site with the group of doctors from SOMOS, I did not go door-to-door and walk around and visit with community members. Instead, we decided that it would be most efficient if we were centralized. We planned for residents to arrive at one place to receive medical checkups, solar lamps, and hand-powered washing machines. I also connected with the town's mayor and his chief of staff, who were able to be there. They made sure everything went as planned and helped distribute items. Incredibly, Coen Vermeer, the founder of Gentlewasher, joined us, traveling all the way from the Netherlands to support the mission. A few weeks before, I had let him know that I was going to distribute more washing machines. He said he was eager to participate and bought his plane tickets!

When I arrived with volunteers, we walked up a hill and saw a huge line of people. I wondered, *What are all these people waiting for?* We made it up the hill and saw the distribution site. In a plaza in front of a church, tents were set up for the medical clinic and for handing out the washing machines and solar lamps. I realized that the line of people was for us, and there were about five hundred people in line. I was struck by the number of people who spent their whole day in line for a solar lamp. *That's how much this means to them*, I realized. Because it meant so much to them, it meant so much to me.

Everyone had been impacted by Hurricane Maria in some shape or form. Everyone. One of the things that I learned from this experience was that while the impact of a storm is not always in our hands, our response is. While I could not control what happened, I *could* control my response, so I chose to respond by helping those around me.

Over time I saw attitudes change in my community. The people I personally knew were more emotionally hurt than physically. I had friends who would tell me that their parents kept arguing because they were stressed. The suicide rate in Puerto Rico went up significantly after Hurricane Maria. Many of my friends did not want to deal with what was going on. They spent their time having bonfires or staying inside with their Xboxes or Netflix. I didn't blame them. They had never experienced anything like this in their lives. But I couldn't ignore the suffering in my community. I had the privilege of having a roof over my head and a family to be with me, and felt it was my responsibility to try to alleviate that suffering.

I am proud of the help I have given my community. I reached thirty-five hundred families in seventeen towns. My interactions with people widened my perspective and gave me a sense of purpose, and I learned that it is so important to be compassionate and to stand up for those around you even in your darkest moments.

What's more: I raised nearly $175,000! I had never done any sort of fundraising, apart from a bake sale in elementary school. I was not in college, I was not a finance major, I was just a normal high school student with a passion and drive to make a difference in the world. I believe that if someone puts their mind to a task, anything is possible. Age is just a number, not a limit to success. If I could touch another person's life and have a positive impact, then anyone else can, too. So don't let anyone say you can't do something until you try. Don't let anyone dim your light.

Continue the Discussion

How strong was Hurricane Maria?

Hurricane Maria was the strongest hurricane to hit the island in over eighty years. It fluctuated between a Category 4 and Category 5 storm. A Category 4 storm has sustained winds that are between 130 and 156 miles per hour; Category 5 storms have winds that are 157 miles per hour or above. When Hurricane Maria made landfall in Puerto Rico, it was a Category 4 storm, because its sustained wind speed was 155 miles per hour. Hurricane Maria also had very heavy rainfall; more than twenty inches of rain fell on Puerto Rico, which led to dangerous flooding.

How much damage did Hurricane Maria cause?

The damage was catastrophic, negatively impacting electrical power, shelter, hospital care, food supply, and more. The power outage that impacted the entire island was one of the largest and worst in U.S. history, and the storm destroyed so many homes that 1.1 million households applied for disaster aid. Sadly, it is estimated that 2,795 people lost their lives because of the hurricane.

Additionally, Hurricane Maria led to

destruction in other places, including the U.S. Virgin Islands and Dominica.

How did Salvador's efforts to help Puerto Rico impact his life?

Salvador saw the power of collaboration and empathy through donations from all around the globe and through the countless people who helped him throughout the process, which empowered and moved him.

During every distribution, he remembered the importance of compassion and standing up for others, even in his darkest moments. As Salvador went door-to-door, the joy and good wishes people gave him sparked in him an unparalleled sense of purpose.

His experience reinvigorated his confidence as a young person with great ideas as well as his belief that goodness and positivity inspires people.

What is Salvador doing now?

Salvador continues to foster climate resilience in communities ridden by natural disasters. After Hurricane Dorian in 2019, he launched a Light and Hope campaign in the Bahamas; after the January 2020 earthquakes, he launched other missions in Puerto Rico.

Apart from advocating for sustainability and climate resilience, Salvador works to promote youth empowerment and makes sure young people have a seat at the table. He is currently a college student.

Get Involved

1. Talk about it.

Talk with your teachers and school officials and encourage them to teach about climate change and its impact as part of the formal education in your school.

2. Read up and speak out.

Join or create a student group that develops awareness about climate change and advocates for sustainable practices within your community. In addition to finding out more about climate change from books and news articles, you can rally friends to join you.

3. Volunteer.

Look around your community and see which groups are having an impact. Groups dedicated to conservation, recycling, or other environmental concerns need hands-on help to achieve their goals of protecting our planet. You may need to team up with a parent or older sibling to volunteer at some places.

Timeline

2017

September 2: Salvador turns fifteen years old.

September 6: Hurricane Irma, a Category 5 hurricane, hits Puerto Rico, causing power outages, major flooding, and structural damage.

September 16: The National Weather Service (NWS) names an impending storm Tropical Storm Maria.

September 17: NWS declares that Tropical Storm Maria has strengthened into a hurricane.

September 19: NWS predicts that Hurricane Maria will be a Category 5 storm; sixty thousand people are still without power due to Hurricane Irma.

Salvador and his family prepare for Hurricane Maria.

September 20: Hurricane Maria makes landfall as a Category 4 storm, causing major destruction and a power outage. The hurricane damages communications, including cell phone, internet, and landline phone service.

Salvador and his family shelter in place in the gym of their apartment building.

September 21: President Trump issues a state of emergency for Puerto Rico, allowing for federal assistance; NWS warns of catastrophic flooding.

September 23: Salvador decides to take action and help Puerto Rico.

September 24: On the day it goes live, Salvador's fundraising campaign receives $14,000.

September 28: More than ten thousand containers of emergency supplies remain docked at a port in San Juan due to road damage and a shortage of drivers and diesel.

September 30: *Teen Vogue* and CNN cover Salvador's fundraiser.

October: Salvador places his first lamp order.

October 1: One of the deadliest mass shootings in U.S. history occurs in Las Vegas.

October 3: Almost two weeks after the hurricane, President Trump visits Puerto Rico.

December 3: Salvador and his team of volunteers head to Loíza and complete their first of many distributions.

December 29: One hundred days after Hurricane Maria, more than a million people do not have power, and hundreds lack drinking water and permanent housing. People in remote areas cannot access health care, because roads are still blocked.

2018

January: Salvador receives hand-powered washing machines, and his fundraiser reaches its $100,000 goal.

August 14: Almost a year after Hurricane Maria, officials declare that power is now restored to the island.

Author's Acknowledgments

If you want to change the world, you need wonderful people to accompany you on the journey. I have been blessed to have found such people. Since I couldn't possibly list everyone who has supported me over the past few years, I have done my best to honor those who have had the most significant impact.

I am extremely grateful to my editors, Dave Eggers, Zainab Nasrati, Zoë Ruiz, and Amanda Uhle, for their tireless work ensuring that what you're reading now is in its best shape. Dave and Amanda, I am forever grateful that fate brought our paths together for the first time in 2018 at the inaugural

International Congress of Youth Voices in San Francisco.

I am deeply indebted to Neha Misra, my guiding light. Neha, without you, your time, and your encouragement, Light and Hope for Puerto Rico could not have gotten off the ground. I am grateful for all the emails and phone calls and for all of the words of wisdom you shared with me to keep me going. Your passions for service and social impact inspired me then, and still do today.

I would not be the same person I am today without my parents, Marta Michelle and Salvador, and my stepdad Ricardo. You guys have inspired, motivated, and encouraged me in all possible ways, and I am eternally grateful for everything you have done to support me. Thank you for teaching me to be humble, joyful, and compassionate.

I will forever appreciate Jean Tirri, my fairy godmother, who has done anything and everything for me. Jean, from lending us a warehouse to store all the lamps and washers to sending me care packages to school, you have always had my back, and I look forward to paying it forward in the future.

I am grateful to my mentor Donald Slater, whose unwavering wisdom and guidance have supported me through the past three years and will continue to do so beyond. Dr. Slater, thank you for always keeping your door open to me, welcoming our fascinating conversations, and giving me a broader perspective of life and our world. Know that my high-fives for the girls will remain a constant as I get older, and I will always be there for them as you have been for me.

I extend my special thanks to my dear friends Alfredo and María Elisa, who participated in nearly every distribution, rain or shine. Even if we had a party the night before, they would wake up at dawn the next morning and show up to the distributions ready to rumble and get the job done.

I want to shout out to all my friends from Andover, whom I cherish deeply. I am grateful for all our hikes to Holt Hill, our late-night runs downtown, our break vacations, and games on the Lawn. Thank you for always being supportive, honest, and willing to have the most insightful conversations with me.

I'd like to recognize my agent Catherine Cuello, who first brought my story to the world. Since day one, she had faith in the mission and put her name on the line to ensure my voice was heard.

I am grateful to all the community leaders for putting in the time and effort to make the distributions possible; they received my initiative with open arms. Amid all of the challenges you all were facing, you were willing to support your community; thank you for sharing the journey with me, house-by-house, mile after mile. Special recognition goes to Lubriel Vega from Morovis and William Santana from Dorado for reaching out to me and maximizing the impact of this effort.

I want to express my gratitude to the nearly thirteen hundred individuals and companies who generously funded Light and Hope for Puerto Rico. Your support was fundamental to ensuring that our efforts could succeed and make a larger impact.

Finally, for all of you who feel that you should've been on this page, please give me a hard time. I promise that when the next book comes around, I won't forget to mention you.

Editors' Acknowledgments

The editors would like to extend special thanks to the Young Editors Project (YEP), which connects young readers to manuscripts in progress. The program gives meaningful opportunities for young people to be part of the professional publishing process and gives authors and publishers meaningful insights into their work. Special thanks to Kitania Folk; Anika Hussain; Aminata from New York City; Ilaria from Trieste, Italy; Julia, Charley, and Noah from Darien, Connecticut; Ty from Warsaw, Poland; Henry from Elsah, Illinois; and from Albuquerque, New

Mexico: Gabriella, Damacio, Rex, Jude, Johnny, Levi, Anna, Jonah, Charlie, Jackson, Bruno, Hunter S., James, Will, Mariella, Max, Munya, Mariana, Joshua, Dylan, Katie, Hunter M., Matrim, Emma, Amadeus, Xavier, Leo, Elliott, Madeline, Sasha, Malia, Luke, Juliet, Evan, Clinton, Isla, Nicholas, Sebastian, Nora, John Paul, Leila, Alexander, Jocelyn, and Karah.

www.youngeditorsproject.org

About I, Witness

I, Witness is a nonfiction book series that tells important stories of real young people who have faced and conquered extraordinary contemporary challenges. There's no better way for young readers to learn about the world's issues and upheavals than through the eyes of young people who have lived through these times.

Proceeds from this book series support the work of the International Alliance of Youth Writing Centers and its sixty-plus member organizations. These nonprofit writing centers are joined in a common belief that young people need places where they can write and be heard, where they can have their voices celebrated and amplified.

www.youthwriting.org